THE MILITARY HISTORY OF WORLD WAR II Volume 13

THE AIR WAR IN THE PACIFIC:
AIR POWER LEADS THE WAY

The Military History of World War II: Volume 13

THE AIR WAR
IN THE PACIFIC
AIR POWER
LEADS THE WAY

by Trevor Nevitt Dupuy
COL., U.S. ARMY, RET.

FRANKLIN WATTS, INC.
575 Lexington Avenue • New York 22

Library of Congress Catalog Card Number: 62-7382
Copyright © 1964 by Franklin Watts, Inc.
Printed in the United States of America

1   2   3   4   5   6   7

Contents

THE MILITARY HISTORY OF WORLD WAR II Volume 13

THE AIR WAR IN THE PACIFIC:
AIR POWER LEADS THE WAY

Japanese troops in Manchuria, 1934.

"The China Incident"

Background

On October 10, 1911, the Chinese people overthrew their last emperor and established a republic. There followed years of turmoil, during which time most of the country was ruled by military men, known as "warlords," who seized power as provincial governors. Neighboring Japan, growing in wealth and power, took advantage of China's weakness to gain influence and control in several coastal regions of the country.

It was not until the 1920's that China found a leader strong and versatile enough to do something about the situation. This was a general named Chiang Kai-shek. Chiang had had military training in Japan, and had also visited Russia, where he had studied the military organization of the Soviet Union. When the president of the new Chinese Republic, Dr. Sun Yat-sen, died in 1925, Chiang's military and political ability made him Dr. Sun's logical successor.

At this time the recognized Chinese government actually controlled only the southeast portion of China. Chiang's first step was to try to unify the strife-torn country. He established peace in most of it by winning a series of victories over the warlords of central and northern China. He then began to try to modernize the country, which had fallen far behind the rest of the world in science, technology, and industry.

Japan watched Chiang's activities with great alarm. The Japanese were afraid that if China became a truly unified and prosperous country, it would be stronger than Japan. Largely because of this fear, they seized the Chinese provinces of Manchuria and Jehol in 1932, and tried to stir up trouble elsewhere in China by supporting people who would oppose Chiang.

Chiang realized that Japan intended to interfere with his plans to unify and strengthen his country, and he knew that this might lead to war. Since Japan had far more powerful military forces than China, Chiang tried to avoid arguments with the Japanese government. At the same time, he tried to strengthen his army and air force with the help of European military advisers. At first he relied on Soviet advisers, but he soon found that these men were trying to force Communism on China. He therefore ordered the Russian military men out of the country, and asked Germany for help in training his army, and Italy for help with his air force.

The Outbreak of War

By 1937, the Japanese realized that they could not undermine the position of Chiang Kai-shek, and they saw that he was steadily strengthening his armed forces. They therefore decided that the only way to keep China from becoming too strong was to conquer the country and make it a colony of Japan, just as they had done with Manchuria and Jehol. On July 7, 1937, Japanese armies invaded north China from their bases in Manchuria.

The Japanese pretended that they were simply sending soldiers into China to "restore order" because Chiang's government was not able to control the country properly. Refusing to admit that their invasion was an act of war, they called it "the China Incident."

In reality, this was the beginning of World War II.

Some of the Japanese armies advanced into north China, while others landed to attack China's great seaport of Shanghai. They were assisted by the modern, efficient Japanese army and navy air forces. Chiang soon realized that the Italians had not done a very good job in building up the Chinese air force, or in training its pilots. Japanese

GROWTH OF THE JAPANESE EMPIRE,

1937–1941

U.S.S.R.

OUTER MONGOLIA

MANCHUKUO

Sakhalin

KURIL IS.

KAMCHATKA

JEHOL

(1937)
PEIPING

KOREA

TIBET

CHINA

(1938)

TOKYO

SHANGHAI (1937)

Wenchow

CHUNGKING

Foochow

Amoy

RYUKYU

Okinawa

EMPIRE

Midway

(1939)

INDIA

BURMA

FR. INDOCHINA

Hong
Kong

Formosa
(1941)

Bonin Is.

Marcus I.

Wake I. (U.S.)

International Date Line

THAILAND

Hainan
(1939)

Andaman Is.

PHILIPPINES
(1940-41)

Spratley Is.

MALAYA

Singapore   Borneo

JAPANESE

MARIANA IS

Guam (U.S.)

Yap   CAROLINE IS.

Palau Is.

Truk

(Japanese Mandate)

MARSHALL IS.

EQUATOR

DUTCH

Sumatra

Java

New
Guinea   Bismarck Arch.

Bougainville   GILBERT IS

SOLOMON IS.

Tulagi   Ellice Is.

EAST

INDIES

DARWIN

AUSTRALIA

Santa Cruz Is.

NEW HEBRIDES   FIJI IS.

■ JAPAN IN 1937
■ JAPANESE EXPANSION

Muddy roads delay the transport of Japanese munitions to the front.

planes quickly shot down the few Chinese aircraft that were able to get into the air. Then, with unchallenged control of the skies, they bombed Chinese airfields and destroyed most of Chiang's remaining aircraft. Following this, they ruthlessly bombed and strafed Chinese cities, trying to terrorize the people so that they would be willing to make peace with Japan.

In desperation Chiang turned again to Soviet Russia for assistance and advice. The Russians sent several squadrons of planes and advisers to help China. Theoretically, these planes were part of the Chinese air force, but in fact the Russian advisers kept them very much under their own control. On the missions which they flew against the Japanese, either in air combat or in attacking Japanese

4

ground forces, the planes were flown by regular Red Air Force officers. They were really using China as a proving ground for their equipment.

Arrival of Chennault

IN THE EARLY SUMMER of 1937, representatives of the Chinese government, still desperately trying to get assistance for the Chinese air force, approached Captain Claire L. Chennault, who was about to retire from the United States Army Air Corps. Chennault was one of the Air Corps' most skilled fighter pilots and a leading expert on tactical air warfare. He was leaving active duty because he was becoming deaf. The Chinese government invited him to become its Adviser on Aeronautical Affairs, with the rank of colonel in the Chinese air force.

A Japanese machine-gun unit moves cautiously forward past two Russian tanks abandoned by the Soviets in fighting along the Mongolian frontier, July, 1939.

Chennault accepted the offer, and soon sailed across the Pacific Ocean to China. When he got there, he discovered how dismally the Italians had failed in their training of Chinese pilots. He tried to help the Chinese in their early air battles against the Japanese, but before long the Chinese air force had practically disappeared, though the Russians were still fighting. Chennault then collected a number of foreign pilots, soldiers of fortune who had volunteered to fight for China in return for high pay. But he soon discovered that these men were not interested in learning his aerial tactics, and also that they were not much interested in fighting. Their main idea seemed to be to have a good time and to get as much money as they could from China without having to take too many risks.

Chennault next began to train some young Chinese pilots in his ideas of aerial fighting. He found that, despite the enthusiasm and courage of many of his young Chinese students, few of them had sufficient technical ability to become pilots. Nevertheless, these Chinese flyers, in cooperation with the Russians, caused the Japanese a great deal of trouble, though they never offered any serious challenge to Japan's control of the air. Then, early in 1939, the Russians left, making the Japanese air force job even easier.

Japanese airplanes ranged far and wide in front of their ground armies advancing into central China from the north and from the eastern seacoast. They repeatedly bombed the large Chinese cities and attacked every defensive position where Chinese troops were trying to hold the Japanese advance. They strafed marching columns of Chinese soldiers with machine-gun fire, and spread terror far and wide by destroying hundreds of China's farm villages.

Learning of Chennault's efforts to build up a new Chinese air force, the Japanese continuously attacked the airfields where the remaining Chinese planes were based. They attempted not only to destroy the

Japanese "Nells."

airfields, but also to terrorize the pilots and ground crews. Chennault realized that he could do nothing unless he could find out when the Japanese planes were on their way. Then he could disperse his planes and send his few good pilots up in the air to fight back.

Chennault decided, therefore, to create an early warning system. He convinced the Chinese government that it should supply very simple radio sets to thousands of patriotic peasants all over China. He then established a central radio control station that could receive reports from these widespread spotters. Whenever Japanese planes took off from airfields in any part of occupied China, Chennault's control station was informed at once. Then, as the Japanese planes passed overhead, his spotters would continue to send reports in to the central station, giving accurate details of numbers, types, and the direction of flight. With this help, Chennault's outmatched Chinese pilots managed to give the skilled Japanese some competition.

But it was still a losing battle. The Japanese spread their control along the entire coast of China, cutting the Chinese government off from most of the overseas sources of the supplies it needed to continue the war. Earlier, the Chinese had been able to get some supplies from Russia, by road across Mongolia and Turkestan. But this assistance stopped when Germany began to threaten Russia early in 1941. Finally, the only remaining link between China and the outside world was along the winding, narrow, mountainous Burma Road, which ran between Lashio, in Burma, and Kunming, in the Chinese province of Yunnan. Chinese trucks could carry only a few supplies over this difficult road, but they were enough to help China keep on fighting.

During 1940 and early 1941, after Germany had defeated France, Japanese forces occupied French Indochina. Defeated France was unable to stop this aggression. The Japanese seized airfields in Indochina, and from these Japanese planes attacked trucks on the Burma Road. Chennault knew that his Chinese pilots could not stop these Japanese attacks, and that it would not be long before the Japanese would be able to cut off almost all of the truck traffic along the Burma Road. If China was to survive, air cover for the road must be provided as soon as possible.

Mission to America

WITH THE APPROVAL OF Generalissimo Chiang Kai-shek, Chennault returned to the United States to try to assemble a group of trained American military flyers who would volunteer to fight for China in return for good pay. While the Chinese government arranged for Lend-Lease shipment of 100 P-40 American fighter planes from the United States, Chennault received unofficial permission from the American government to recruit volunteers from among active and recently discharged American military pilots. By the summer of 1941, he had enlisted about 90 young volunteers who had Army, Navy, or Marine Corps flying experience. In addition, he had about 150 qualified mechanics and administrative men to serve as the ground support element of this newly established American Volunteer Group — or AVG, as it was called.

Chennault then obtained permission from the British government to use an idle British air base at Toungoo, in south-central Burma, as a training base. Here, during the late summer and early fall of 1941, the American airmen, ground crews, and the P-40 airplanes were gathered. During the next three months, Chennault taught his young pilots to fly and fight together as a team, using his own system of combat. Although they were all trained flyers, they had never worked together, and they were not familiar with Chennault's system. Furthermore, they were acquainted with neither Japanese aircraft, nor Japanese methods of aerial fighting. Chennault knew them both very well by now. He told his men that the Japanese airmen were good, but he trained his pilots to take advantage of enemy weaknesses. By early December the members of the AVG had developed into a splendid fighting team.

During this training period, some AVG pilots decided to paint eyes and a row of teeth on the engines of their P-40's, which made the planes look like tiger sharks. Chennault approved of this, and soon all of the planes were decorated with eyes and teeth. Soon someone began to call the group "The Flying Tigers," and the name stuck.

On December 8th,* Chennault and his men learned of the Japa-
* December 7th, east of the International Date Line.

9

Wrecked U.S. planes at Wheeler Air Base after the Japanese attack on Pearl Harbor.

nese attacks on Pearl Harbor, Hong Kong, and Malaya. At the same time, Japanese troops began to move into Thailand. With this increasing Japanese activity in Southeast Asia, Chennault felt sure that the Japanese would move soon against the Burma Road. He therefore shifted two of his three groups to Kunming. The other he kept at Toungoo, and awaited further developments.

Japanese Air Power Sweeps the Seas

Japanese Plans

DURING THE EARLY autumn of 1941, relations between the United States and Japan had grown increasingly tense. President Roosevelt

10

had warned the Japanese against making further moves against China, or in Southeast Asia. The United States had stepped up its Lend-Lease assistance to China over the Burma Road. And President Roosevelt had stopped all American trade with Japan. The American government was trying to make Japan realize that a continuation of her aggressive expansion in Asia would mean war with the United States.

The Japanese did not want to fight America, but they had no intention of stopping their plans for establishing what they called the "Greater East Asia Co-prosperity Sphere," by which Japan would completely control China and Southeast Asia. American threats and economic pressure simply made the Japanese all the more determined to press ahead with their plans of conquest and to seize all of the rich territories of Southeast Asia — the so-called "Southern Resources Area." Once this was accomplished, they believed they would be self-sufficient in the raw materials and manufactured goods they had previously been buying from America.

Thus, while Japanese envoys were negotiating with the American government in Washington, the Japanese government in Tokyo was completing preparations for war. The details were worked out by Japanese Imperial Headquarters, which was composed of the combined army and navy staffs. Chief of the Army General Staff was General Hajime Sugiyama; Chief of the Naval General Staff was Admiral of the Fleet Osami Nagano. Overall control and direction were exercised by General Hideki Tojo, who was the prime minister of Japan, and who made decisions in the event of disagreement between the army and navy chiefs.

The Japanese plan provided for simultaneous land and naval attacks in several directions at once. Japan planned amphibious invasions of the British colony of Malaya, and of the American-owned

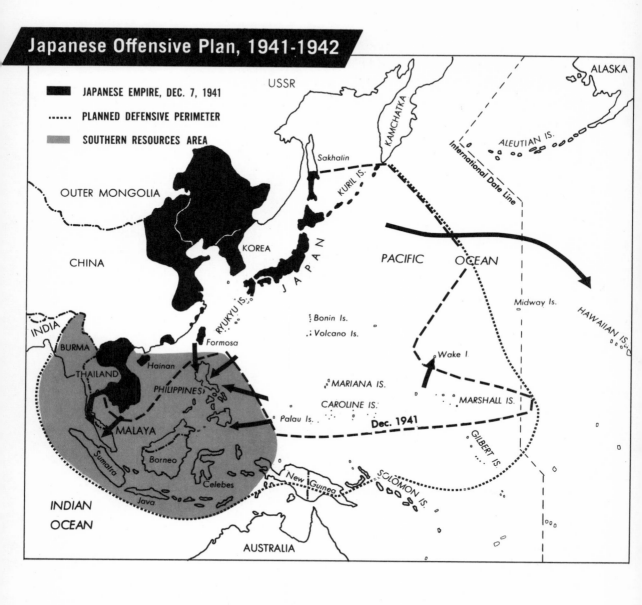

Japanese Offensive Plan, 1941-1942

JAPANESE EMPIRE, DEC. 7, 1941

...... **PLANNED DEFENSIVE PERIMETER**

SOUTHERN RESOURCES AREA

ALASKA

USSR

KAMCHATKA

Sakhalin

ALEUTIAN IS.

International Date Line

KURIL IS.

OUTER MONGOLIA

KOREA

CHINA

JAPAN

PACIFIC OCEAN

Midway Is.

HAWAIIAN IS.

RYUKYU IS.

Bonin Is.

Volcano Is.

Wake I.

INDIA

BURMA

Formosa

Hainan

THAILAND

PHILIPPINES

MARIANA IS.

MARSHALL IS.

CAROLINE IS.

Palau Is.

Dec. 1941

GILBERT IS.

MALAYA

Sumatra

Borneo

Celebes

New Guinea

SOLOMON IS.

Java

INDIAN OCEAN

AUSTRALIA

Philippine Islands. Then, from bases in Malaya and the Philippines, they intended to continue on to seize the Netherlands East Indies. At the same time, other army units would occupy the weak neutral country of Thailand, in preparation for an invasion of Burma, while smaller army and navy forces would seize the British colony of Hong Kong, and the American island possessions of Guam and Wake islands.

The signal to start all these attacks would be given by the main striking force of the Japanese navy. Six aircraft carriers would transport the First Air Fleet, which was to launch a surprise attack against the United States Pacific Fleet at Pearl Harbor. By destroying or severely damaging that fleet, the Japanese would be sure to prevent any possible interference with their planned invasion of the "Southern Resources Area."

Once they had seized this area, the Japanese planned to establish a defensive perimeter of island strongholds in the Central and Southwest Pacific, to frustrate any efforts by Britain and America to recover the conquered regions. The Japanese leaders believed this perimeter would be so strong that the Allies would soon become discouraged and make peace.

Their operations in China and their observation of German *blitzkrieg* in Europe had taught both the Japanese army and navy the importance of air power in support of surface operations. Accordingly, the Japanese had put much emphasis on the development of their army and their navy air forces. Their plan provided for violent air attack to start each of their offensive operations. And when they had completed their conquests, they expected to rely upon air power, sea power, and powerful land garrisons to hold their island outposts, and to halt any Allied attacks on their defensive perimeter.

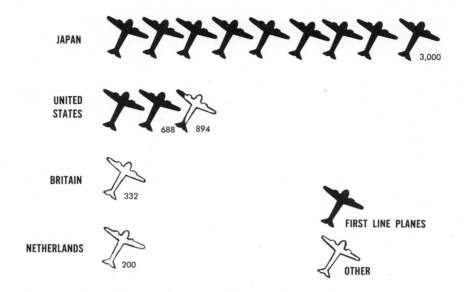

(IN THE PACIFIC)

JAPAN   3,000

UNITED STATES   688   894

BRITAIN   332

NETHERLANDS   200

FIRST LINE PLANES

OTHER

Comparison of Air Forces

By December of 1941, the Japanese army and navy air forces both consisted of about 1,500 first-line aircraft. The navy had about 3,500 trained pilots, the army about 2,500; these first-line pilots all had more than 500 hours' flying experience, and most of them had had some combat service in China. The 600 pilots in the navy aircraft carrier groups were probably the best trained and most skillful in the world. By December, 1941, in order to build up these air forces and to replace losses, Japanese factories were turning out about 425 planes per month. New pilots were being trained at the rate of 2,750 a year. After the war began, Japan greatly increased the rate of construction of new planes, and also speeded up her pilot training programs.

At this time, the largest concentration of non-Japanese military force in the Pacific Ocean was at the American stronghold of Oahu, in Hawaii. Here, at Pearl Harbor, was based the U.S. Pacific Fleet. The base was protected by an Army garrison of nearly 50,000 soldiers, plus 231 Army Air Force planes and about 170 land-based Navy planes. Of these, however, only 162 of the Army planes were modern combat aircraft. But there were almost 180 first-line planes on the Pacific Fleet's two carriers. (A third carrier was being repaired on the west coast of the United States.)

Elsewhere in the Pacific, there were 12 Marine Corps fighter planes and 12 Navy patrol bombers on Midway Island, and 12 more Marine fighters on tiny Wake Island. In the Philippines the Far Eastern Air

This print, captured on Attu, shows a group of Japanese naval aviators.

U.S. NAVY DEPARTMENT

Force, under Major General Lewis H. Brereton, had 277 aircraft, but of these only 107 P-40 fighters and 35 B-17 "Flying Fortresses" were first-line fighting planes. In the Netherlands East Indies the Dutch had about 200 aircraft, mostly old, slow models. In Malaya and Singapore Air Chief Marshal Sir Robert Brooke-Popham had 332 British and Australian aircraft. Most of the Royal Air Force pilots had had combat experience, and were probably as good as the Japanese, but their planes were old, and no match for Japanese aircraft.

In fact, only the most modern British and American fighter planes could compete with the fast, light, Japanese "Zero" or "Zeke" fighters. Britain could not spare any of her Hurricanes or Spitfires from the war against Germany and Italy, while the United States had only a total of 233 of the new American P-40 "Tomahawks" in the Philippines and Hawaii. And neither these, nor the Navy F4F "Wildcat" carrier fighter planes, could keep up in a dogfight with the faster-climbing, more maneuverable Japanese Zeros.

The only important advantage that American fighter planes had over similar Japanese types was in their heavier, more rugged construction, and in the armor plate protection built around the pilot's seat. Because of this, the American planes could take much more punishment than could the Japanese aircraft from the guns of enemy fighter planes and from antiaircraft fire. The Japanese planes would often fly apart or fall out of control after a few hits. But because their planes were so much faster and more maneuverable, the Japanese pilots counted on receiving fewer hits than the Americans.

The new American B-17 Flying Fortresses were bigger, were better armed, and had a longer range than the best Japanese bombers. But very few of these had been built or put into air units by December of 1941. There were only forty-seven in the Pacific area.

By December of 1941, the overall combined strength of the United

States Army Air Corps and the Navy's air arm was slightly over 2,000 first-line, modern combat aircraft. These were about equally divided between the two services. More than 3,000 additional but outmoded fighting planes were also in service in Army and Navy units. These were no match for either German or Japanese planes. The Army had about 9,000 trained pilots, the Navy nearly 6,000. But most of the American planes and pilots were on training programs in the United States, or in units preparing for war against Germany, which now seemed probable.

Pearl Harbor

ON NOVEMBER 26, 1941, the Japanese First Air Fleet, consisting of 414 planes and 6 aircraft carriers, escorted by 2 battleships and 12 other warships, left Hitokappu Bay, in the Kurile Islands, to steam silently eastward into the North Pacific Ocean. Commanding the fleet was Vice Admiral Chuichi Nagumo. His objective was the American Pacific Fleet at Pearl Harbor.

In Washington, meanwhile, two Japanese ambassadors carried out Premier Tojo's orders to pretend to continue negotiations with the United States. Because of this diplomatic treachery, because of the skill and caution with which Nagumo's fleet approached Hawaii from the northwest, and because of lack of alertness on the part of the Army and Navy commanders in Oahu, the Americans had no idea of the Japanese threat to their principal Pacific stronghold. They were totally unprepared to protect themselves.

Because United States code experts had succeeded in deciphering the Japanese radio codes, American military leaders believed that war would break out around December 7 or December 8. But they had fixed their whole attention on the South China Sea, where large

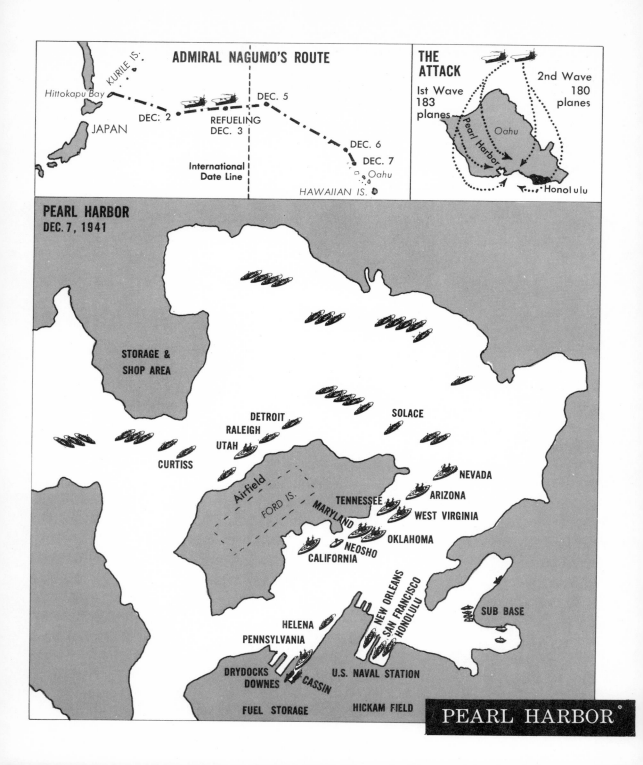

PEARL HARBOR

convoys of Japanese troopships, and numerous Japanese warships were very active. They completely ignored the possibility of a Japanese attack against Pearl Harbor. Although the Japanese did not know that the Americans were reading their radio messages, Nagumo's First Air Fleet kept complete radio silence, so that its location would not be detected by American radio direction finders.

At dawn on Sunday, December 7, the first wave of 189 attack planes took off from the Japanese carriers, 230 miles north of Oahu. As they headed toward the coast of Oahu, the pilots heard the Honolulu radio station reporting weather conditions over the island.

At 7:55 A.M., the first of 50 horizontal bombers struck at the row of American battleships moored in Pearl Harbor, just as 45 fighters swept down to strafe and bomb the Navy and Army Air Force fields on the island of Oahu. Immediately after this, 40 torpedo bombers came in to strike the battleships, doing great damage; these were followed by more horizontal bombers and 54 dive bombers.

Most of the American planes were lined up on their airfields, where they made easy targets for the Japanese fighters. A handful of Army and Navy planes were able to take the air during the thirty-five minutes of the first attack, but they offered little opposition to the efficient Japanese. Only three Japanese planes were shot down by American defensive fighters, and six more were lost to antiaircraft fire from the ships where, despite the total surprise of the attack, American sailors took their battle stations with amazing speed.

In the middle of the raid, twelve unarmed B-17 Flying Fortresses, on their way to the Philippines from the American west coast, flew unexpectedly into the Japanese formations. The Japanese, almost as surprised as the American bomber crews, attacked at once. The B-17's made emergency landings at various fields on Oahu — one on a golf course. All reached the ground, but the Japanese fighters then destroyed one bomber, and seriously damaged two more.

19

The first Japanese attack caused tremendous damage to the Fleet and started fires all over Oahu. The stunned Americans, barely over the shock and dismay, were caring for the hundreds of wounded when a second Japanese wave of 171 planes struck at 9:00 A.M. The second attack, though unexpected, did not cause the same kind of shock as the first one. More American Navy and Army fighter planes got in the air. Helped by antiaircraft fire, they knocked down 20 Japanese planes. About the same number of American planes were shot down by the Japanese during the confused fighting over the island. Despite this interference, however, the Japanese planes pressed their attacks vigorously against ground targets and added to the damage they had already done. The last attacking plane turned northward to rejoin Nagumo's fleet at 9:45. The Japanese had lost 29 aircraft and

Firemen prepare to attempt to extinguish the oil flames following the Japanese bombing of Hickam Field, December 7, 1941.

55 flyers during the fighting. Several damaged planes crash-landed on the carrier decks.

In one hour and fifty minutes the Japanese had inflicted terrible losses upon the defending forces of Oahu. A total of 2,403 men were killed, 1,178 were wounded. Five battleships were sunk or were in sinking condition, and the other three were all damaged sufficiently to be out of action for three months or more. Three destroyers were also sunk, as well as two other fleet vessels. Three cruisers and two fleet support ships were badly damaged. Nearly 100 Navy planes were destroyed, while the Army lost 152 of its aircraft. Most of these planes were hit on the ground.

The striking power of the United States Pacific Fleet — with the important exception of the two aircraft carriers — was smashed. The Japanese had taught the United States, and the rest of the world as well, the potentialities of air power — particularly of carrier-based air power.

The Prince of Wales *and the* Repulse

BEFORE DAWN on December 8,* while planes that had struck Pearl Harbor were still landing on Nagumo's carriers, other Japanese aircraft were striking Royal Air Force bases in Malaya. These attacks were immediately followed by amphibious landings along the seacoast of northeastern Malaya. Late on December 8, Admiral Sir Tom Philipps, commanding the British Far Eastern Fleet, decided to strike against the Japanese convoys and beachheads. He sailed from Singapore with the battleship HMS *Prince of Wales*, the battle cruiser HMS *Repulse*, and an escort of four destroyers.

* At 10:00 A.M., December 7, in Hawaii, it was 4:00 A.M., December 8, in Malaya, west of the International Date Line.

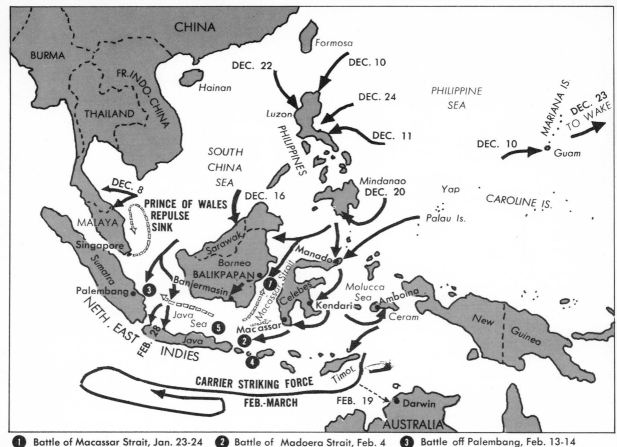

1 Battle of Macassar Strait, Jan. 23-24   2 Battle of Madoera Strait, Feb. 4   3 Battle off Palembang, Feb. 13-14
4 Battle of Lombok Strait, Feb. 19-20   5 Battle of the Java Sea, Feb. 27-28

Because of the damage caused by the early Japanese air strikes, and because of the need to defend Malaya and Singapore with the surviving planes, the RAF was unable to provide any air cover for the British naval squadron. Admiral Philipps, however, felt confident that he could smash the convoys, then return safely to Singapore before Japanese air units could concentrate against his big ships.

22

The British squadron arrived off the Japanese landing beaches late on December 9, to find that the troop transports had already unloaded their troops and fled northward. After an unsuccessful search for the convoys, Philipps' ships were returning to Singapore late the next morning when they were attacked by a force of sixty-one torpedo planes and twenty-seven light bombers, based in southern Indochina. Despite British evasive maneuvers and intense antiaircraft fire, the Japanese skillfully and persistently pressed their attacks. Within two hours both the *Prince of Wales* and *Repulse* were sunk; only three or four Japanese planes had been shot down. More than one thousand British sailors were killed or drowned, including Admiral Philipps.

This was the first time in history that battleships at sea had been sunk by air attack. By destroying the only two Allied capital ships in the Far East, the Japanese had won complete freedom of movement in the waters around Southeast Asia. In slightly over two days, Japanese air power had destroyed or put out of action ten Allied capital ships, with the loss of only thirty-two Japanese planes. Japanese air power had gained control of the Pacific Ocean, from Pearl Harbor to Singapore.

Allies on the Defensive

Defeat of the Far Eastern Air Force

AT MANILA in the Philippines, General MacArthur's headquarters received word of the Japanese attack on Pearl Harbor several hours before dawn on December 8. General Brereton's Far Eastern Air Force headquarters at Clark Field was immediately informed. Both

MacArthur and Brereton apparently considered the possibility of getting the jump on the Japanese by sending their thirty-five B-17 Flying Fortresses on a raid against airfields on Formosa, but before an attack could be made, an air reconnaissance was necessary. While one of the B-17's was making this scouting trip, MacArthur ordered Brereton to make the attack as soon as he was ready. Early that same morning, General H. H. Arnold, commanding the United States Army Air Corps, made a long distance telephone call from Washington to warn Brereton to be alert and fully prepared for Japanese bombing attacks from Formosa.

Accordingly, early in the morning, American patrol planes took off from their fields to search for the expected Japanese bombers. During much of the morning, most of the remaining planes were in the air, so they would not be caught by a surprise attack. Only a few Japanese planes appeared, however, and these the American planes quickly chased away. The Americans did not realize that the Japanese had in fact planned an early morning attack against the Philippines, but that their planes on Formosa had been grounded by early morning fog. By 10:00 A.M., however, the fog began to lift on Formosa, and about two hundred Japanese planes headed toward Luzon.

The Americans were new at this business of war. Noontime came, and since no Japanese attack forces had appeared, the American planes returned to their fields and the pilots went to their mess halls for lunch, leaving the planes lined up, ready for a quick takeoff. Many radio and telephone operators were also at lunch, and so, for these and other more obscure reasons, early warning radar reports of the approach of the Japanese planes did not reach Clark Field, where most of the American planes were stationed. Brereton had issued no orders to have the planes dispersed, and had made no arrangements for air cover or patrol during the lunch hour. Apparently there was no plan for urgent transmission of alert warnings from the radar sites.

When the Japanese planes arrived over Clark Field, shortly after noon, their pilots were amazed to find the American planes lined up on the field. Quickly they attacked. The explosion of the bombs was the first warning heard by the Americans in their mess halls. In the following hour of horror, a few fighter planes got off the ground, to fight heroically against overwhelming numbers of Japanese Zeros. But nothing could replace the eighteen B-17's and fifty-three P-40's destroyed in the first few minutes. Practically all of the rest of the planes were damaged. Only seven Japanese planes were shot down.

Despite the example of the attack on Pearl Harbor, despite alert orders from MacArthur and Arnold, and despite their own early morning alertness, lack of experience — and amazing lack of preparation — had caused the American airmen to make a tragic error. As a result, they lost half of their first-line planes. They also lost whatever chance they had for retaining air superiority over the Philippines.

Preliminary Japanese landings on northern Luzon began on December 10. On December 18, Japanese army planes were moved to bases on the northern and northwest coast of Luzon from which they were able to give direct support to the main Japanese landing at Lingayan Gulf on December 22. By this time Japanese planes completely controlled the air over Luzon. The few remaining American bombers had been withdrawn to fields in Mindanao. Later, they were pulled further back, to Australia.

Japanese Air Power on the Offensive

WITH THE ASSISTANCE of vigorous bombing and strafing by their supporting air units, the skilled Japanese jungle fighters advanced quickly both in Malaya and Luzon. Every time they captured an

Allied airfield, Japanese engineers quickly repaired bomb damage, or the destruction created by the retreating Allies, and then flew their own planes in. From these advance bases the Japanese planes were able to give continuing close and effective support to the ground troops. Even the long delay caused by determined American defense of Bataan and Corregidor did not stop the Japanese advance elsewhere. Singapore surrendered on February 15, 1942.

Meanwhile, early in January 1942, a coordinated Japanese naval and land advance into the Netherlands East Indies had begun, under the cover of land-based and carrier aircraft. The outnumbered, outmatched Allied planes were able to accomplish little. Each time the Japanese took another base, they rushed in more planes. Their air control stretched farther and farther southward into Indonesia.

By mid-February, the Japanese had established themselves in eastern Sumatra, on the southeast corner of Borneo, and in southern Celebes; farther east they had captured the Dutch naval base at Amboina. Japanese control of the air by this time was so complete that on February 19 Admiral Nagumo's carrier fleet steamed without opposition into the Timor Sea to strike a devastating blow at the main Allied base at Port Darwin, in northwestern Australia. They destroyed docks and warehouses, and sank all the ships in the harbor. The Japanese carriers then moved south of Java, to hammer the main Allied naval base of Surabaya in cooperation with land-based planes from Borneo and Celebes. These planes then provided cover and support to the Japanese naval squadrons that smashed the last organized Allied naval resistance in Indonesia in the Battle of the Java Sea on February 27.

Japanese troops then landed on the island of Java itself. On March 9, Dutch resistance ended. Other Japanese troops had already occupied Rabaul, in Britain's Admiralty Islands, and had seized Lae and

Salamaua in northeastern New Guinea. Japan controlled the whole Southwest Pacific. Australia and New Zealand were now in the war zone.

Japanese Carriers in the Indian Ocean

IN LATE MARCH, Admiral Nagumo's carriers, which had smashed Pearl Harbor and Port Darwin, swept into the Indian Ocean, escorted by four fast, modern battleships and numerous other warships. A British fleet, built around five old battleships, and commanded by Vice Admiral Sir James Somerville, steamed out to meet them. Fortunately for the outmatched British, the two fleets passed each other at sea, several hundred miles apart.

On April 5, more than two hundred Japanese carrier planes hit the British naval base of Colombo, and were met by about sixty RAF fighters. A violent air battle took place over southwestern Ceylon, with each side losing about twenty-five planes. Later that same day, Japanese dive bombers sank two British heavy cruisers that were trying to join Somerville's fleet, which was refueling at Addu Atoll.

Early next morning the Japanese struck along the coast of south India, damaging shore installations and sinking coastal shipping. This was repeated the two following days. Then on April 9, the carrier planes returned to Ceylon, this time to strike the naval base at Trincomalee. Once again the RAF was waiting. The British pilots shot down fifteen attacking planes, and lost eleven of their own. At the same time a few British light bombers attacked the carriers, but most of these bombers were lost in vain efforts to get past the screen of defensive Japanese fighters.

For the next three days, Japanese carrier planes raided far northward into the Bay of Bengal and along the southeastern coast of

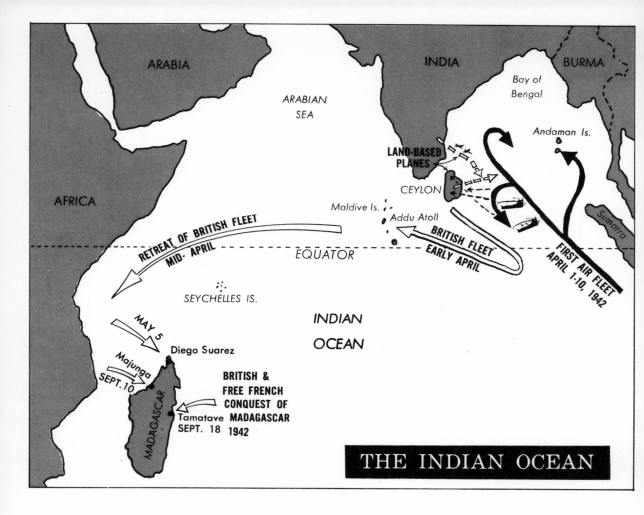

THE INDIAN OCEAN

India. They sank a light aircraft carrier, a destroyer, and many merchant ships, and also damaged shore installations. RAF opposition continued to be fierce, however, and by April 9, Admiral Nagumo had lost almost a third of his planes. He therefore decided to return to the Pacific in order to give his hardworking carrier air groups a rest and to provide them with replacements.

Meanwhile, Somerville had been ordered to withdraw his outmatched fleet to the east coast of Africa. Thus, in addition to controlling the waters of the Central and Western Pacific, the Japanese had also established their supremacy in the central and eastern Indian Ocean. They had accomplished this by skillful, aggressive, and devastating use of air power. In particular, they had proven to the world that they had the most effective carrier striking force in the world.

Rays in the Allied Gloom

Allied Strategy

SHORTLY AFTER Pearl Harbor, Prime Minister Churchill, President Roosevelt, and their military advisers met in Washington to establish a common strategy for carrying on simultaneous wars against Germany and Japan. They agreed that the top military leadership in the war should be exercised by a Combined Chiefs of Staff Committee consisting of the top military officers of the United States and Britain. This was a seven-man group made up of the three members of the British Chiefs of Staff Committee — the senior officers of the British Army, Royal Navy, and Royal Air Force — and the four-man American Joint Chiefs of Staff: General George C. Marshall, Army Chief of Staff; Admiral Ernest J. King, Chief of Naval Operations; General Henry H. Arnold, Chief of the Army Air Force, and Admiral William D. Leahy, Personal Chief of Staff to the President.

At their first meeting, in Washington, Roosevelt, Churchill, and the Combined Chiefs of Staff reached a number of decisions on Allied strategy. The most important was an agreement that America and Britain would first concentrate their efforts against Germany. Once

Germany had been defeated, then they would throw all of their military might against Japan. Meanwhile, they would stay on the defensive in the Pacific Ocean and on the continent of Asia, simply trying to halt the Japanese offensives, and keeping open lines of communication to Hawaii, Australia, New Zealand, India, and China.

The British and American leaders also divided responsibility for supervising the worldwide war effort. Operations in Europe and the Atlantic Ocean would be run directly by the full seven-man Combined Chiefs of Staff Committee. Operations in the Pacific Ocean would be handled by the American Joint Chiefs of Staff, while the British Chiefs of Staff would be responsible for operations in the Middle East, in the Indian Ocean, and in Southeast Asia. The Americans would assume principal responsibility for Allied support to China.

The Flying Tigers

THE COMBINED CHIEFS OF STAFF were still meeting in Washington in December, 1941, when the Japanese began a massive aerial attack on the British colony of Burma. They concentrated their blows against the seaport of Rangoon, the key link between China's Burma Road and the outside world. The Japanese had not expected much opposition in these raids over Burma, since they knew that the few old RAF planes in Burma were no match for their newer and more numerous planes. But they had not counted on the presence of Colonel Chennault's American Volunteer Group.

Because Burma had no adequate air warning net, Chennault had sent two of his three AVG squadrons north to Kunming, to protect the Burma Road. His third squadron he sent to an RAF base at Mingaladon, near Rangoon. Both portions of his group soon had a chance to demonstrate the quality of his training, and of his aerial combat methods.

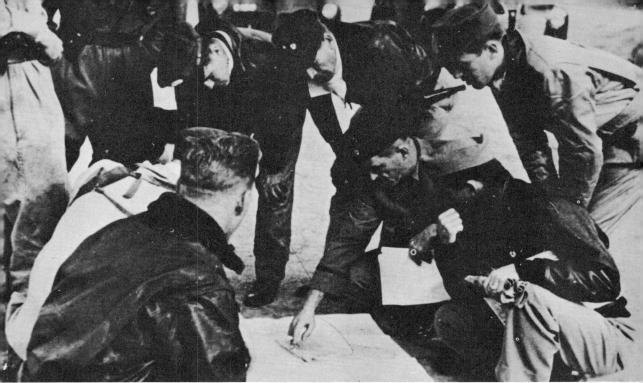

General Claire Chennault points out a target to some of his "Flying Tiger" pilots.

U.S. OFFICE OF WAR INFORMATION

On December 19, Chennault's efficient Chinese air warning net reported Japanese planes heading toward Kunming from northern Indochina. The Flying Tigers scrambled into the air, and a few minutes later shot down nine of ten approaching Japanese bombers. One American pilot chased the surviving Japanese plane too far, and ran out of gas before he could get back to Kunming airfield. But though his plane crashed, he was able to walk back and rejoin the group. It was many months before the Japanese tried another attack on Kunming.

Activity in Burma began with a Japanese raid of fifty-four bombers and twenty-four fighters against Rangoon on December 23. Without an air warning net, the Americans and the RAF planes at Mingaladon did not learn of the attack until Japanese bombs were falling on the field and hitting the Rangoon docks. Taking off under fire, however, the Americans shot down six Japanese planes, while losing two of their own.

In the following days the Flying Tigers kept planes constantly in the air so as to be ready for Japanese air strikes. The attacks came in great numbers, and the Americans took a heavy toll while losing few planes themselves. In later attacks, the Japanese reduced the number of bombers and increased the number of escorting fighters in an effort to try to beat off the AVG and RAF fighters. But the story continued to be the same. By February 12, the Flying Tigers had shot down nearly one hundred Japanese planes, and had damaged many more. They had lost fifteen of their own planes, but nine of the shot-down

Air group in the Aleutians.

A Flying Tiger pilot mounts his plane for a takeoff somewhere in China.

pilots had made their way back to the base to fly again. The RAF planes were not so good as the rugged American P-40's, and their pilots did not have the advantage of Chennault's superb training and tactical combat system. Most of the fighting burden fell on the Americans.

To rest his pilots, and to repair their worn-out or damaged airplanes, Chennault rotated each of his three squadrons through the fighting around Rangoon, always keeping two squadrons at Kunming. When they were not fighting off Japanese air attacks, the Flying Tigers and RAF planes from Mingaladon tried to help British ground troops stop the Japanese overland invasion from Thailand. But even with this help the British soldiers could not stop the enemy advance. Even the arrival of Chinese troops from Yunnan did not halt the Japanese.

Japanese aviator.

Constant operations against the enemy in the air and on the ground quickly wore out the British and American aircraft. By the end of February, there were only nine AVG planes and six RAF aircraft serviceable at Mingaladon. On February 26 and 27, the nine American planes shot down more than twenty Japanese, without any loss themselves. Then, as Japanese ground troops approached, Chennault shifted his Burma base north to the RAF field at Magwe.

Singapore had fallen on February 15, and by the beginning of March, Japanese air units in Malaya had come north to join in the invasion of Burma. Nevertheless, despite the appearance of hundreds of Japanese planes over the battlefields, the Flying Tigers continued

34

to take a heavy toll of the attackers, with very few losses themselves. And in addition to intercepting Japanese bombing raids, the American flyers took every opportunity to provide ground support to the hard-pressed British and Chinese troops on the ground.

On March 21, however, the Japanese took advantage of the lack of an adequate Allied air warning net in Burma. In a massive bombing attack on the RAF and Flying Tiger base at Magwe, they destroyed effective Allied air power in Burma. Remnants of the British air units withdrew to bases in India. Chennault reluctantly ordered his three surviving planes to fly back to a new base he had established at Loiwing, at the Burma-China border. The other pilots and ground crews went back by truck along the Burma Road. The Flying Tigers continued to support the ground troops fighting in Burma, but their base was now so far away that they could spend relatively little time over the battlefield, and were rarely in position to intercept Japanese bombing raids.

During April, the Allied efforts to defend Burma collapsed under a series of powerful Japanese ground and air attacks. By the end of May, the remnants of the Allied armies had been driven from Burma. The Burma Road supply line was cut; China was isolated from her allies.

The Raid from Shangri-La

NEWSPAPER REPORTS on the feats of the Flying Tigers had given some encouragement to Americans and Britons who had had so much bad news during that awful winter of 1941-42. But what the Flying Tigers did to the Japanese in Burma was very minor indeed to what the Japanese were doing to the British and Americans and Dutch elsewhere in Southeast Asia and across the Pacific Ocean.

35

In April, however, as the Allied front was collapsing in Burma, the American Navy and the Army Air Force were making plans to strike back.

This was to be a blow against Japan itself. The Japanese main islands were far beyond the range of any American bombing plane from any base that America still held in the Pacific. But the aircraft carrier USS *Hornet* was to carry a group of sixteen Army B-25's deep into the Western Pacific, to within 500 miles of Tokyo. The planes, under the command of Lieutenant Colonel James H. Doolittle, would then take off from the carrier and fly to central Japan, where they would drop bombs on Tokyo and other cities. They would then continue on to land on airfields in Nationalist China.

The American leaders realized that this would be only a pinprick against Japan. But they knew that any effort to strike back against the enemy would encourage the American people, and would give new heart to Allied fighting men who were taking such a terrible beating elsewhere.

In mid-April, a small task force built around the carrier USS *Enterprise* and commanded by Vice Admiral William F. Halsey, Jr., met the *Hornet* in the Central Pacific to provide air and surface protection for the carrier and her bombers. On April 18 the task force was about 700 miles east of Japan when it was sighted by a Japanese patrol vessel. The American ships quickly sank the Japanese boat, but not before she had sent out a radio message reporting their location.

Halsey and Doolittle knew that they were still too far away from Japan for the planes to fly to their targets and continue on to the airfields in China without refueling. Furthermore, the sea was so very rough at that time that even the best-trained Navy carrier pilots would have had difficulty flying off in their small planes. The Army pilots had had no training for such takeoffs and, moreover, their

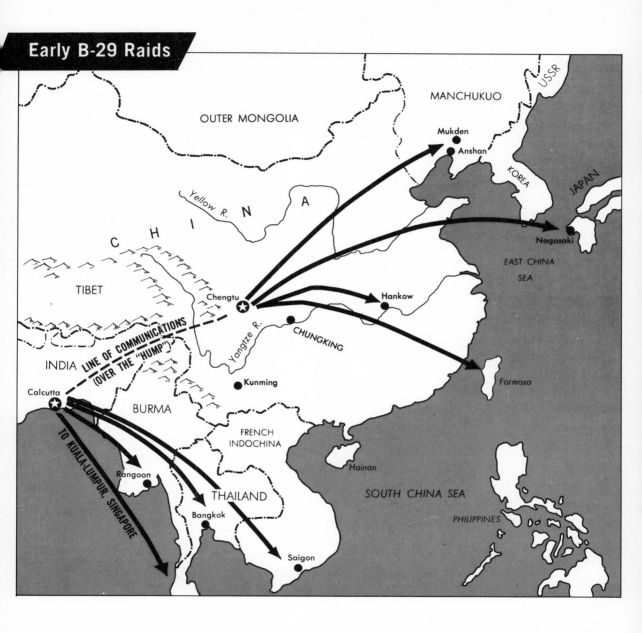

Early B-29 Raids

OUTER MONGOLIA

MANCHUKUO

USSR

Mukden

Anshan

KOREA

JAPAN

Yellow R.

C H I N A

Nagasaki

EAST CHINA

SEA

TIBET

Chengtu

Hankow

Yangtze R.

CHUNGKING

Formosa

LINE OF COMMUNICATIONS

(OVER THE "HUMP")

INDIA

Kunming

Calcutta

BURMA

TO KUALA-LUMPUR, SINGAPORE

Rangoon

FRENCH

INDOCHINA

Hainan

THAILAND

Bangkok

SOUTH CHINA SEA

PHILIPPINES

Saigon

bombers were much larger than regular carrier planes. Nevertheless, Doolittle and his pilots were determined to make their attack. Despite the pitching carrier deck, all of the big, heavily loaded bombers took off safely.

Doolittle and his planes arrived over Japan about noon, just as Tokyo was having a practice air raid alert. No one on the ground, and none of the Japanese pilots in the air, noticed the arrival of the Americans until bombs began to drop on the city. Actually, there were so few bombs from so few planes, and Tokyo was such a big city, that the explosives did very little damage. But the very fact that the Americans had been able to strike Tokyo, and to hit other cities as well, dismayed the Japanese. The news of the raid caused great rejoicing in Allied countries.

With their gas tanks almost empty, the American planes continued westward over the Sea of Japan toward China. One landed safely near Vladivostok on the east coast of Soviet Siberia, where plane and crew were interned by the neutral Russians. All of the other planes crash-landed in eastern China. Nevertheless, of the eighty men who took part in the mission, only nine were killed in these crashes, though several more were seriously injured. Some of the survivors, however, were captured by the Japanese, and a few were brutally executed.

Although the fact that Americans had bombed Japan was published in American newspapers, how the planes had gotten to Japan was a closely guarded secret. It was not certain whether the Japanese were aware that the bombers had taken off from the carrier they had sighted on the morning of April 18. The Americans, naturally, did not want to give the Japanese any more information than necessary. A few days later a newspaperman asked President Roosevelt where the American raid had started from. Roosevelt replied: "From Shangri-La."

Battle of the Coral Sea

ONE RESULT of the Doolittle raid against Tokyo was to convince the Japanese that they should extend their defensive perimeter farther east. They decided to seize bases in the Aleutian Islands and to capture Midway in the Central Pacific, so as to make it more difficult for American aircraft carriers to penetrate into the Western Pacific Ocean and to attack Japan. This would also enable the Japanese to interfere with American activities in Hawaii and the Eastern Pacific.

First, however, the Japanese planned to seize southern New Guinea and the southern Solomon Islands, so as to get bases from which to attack the line of communications over the Pacific from

A U.S. bomber makes a pinpoint hit on a cluster of Japanese Army barracks outside of Tokyo during the Doolittle raid on Japan.

OFFICIAL U.S. AIR FORCE PHOTO

America to Australia. Early in May, a small force seized Tulagi, in the southern Solomons. A larger expedition then sailed in a convoy from Rabaul into the Coral Sea, heading for Port Moresby, in southern Papua, New Guinea. Two naval task forces, including three aircraft carriers and other warships, protected the convoy.

Since the Americans were still reading secret Japanese messages, Admiral Nimitz knew all about the Japanese plans. He ordered Vice Admiral Frank J. Fletcher to the Coral Sea with a task force consisting of the carriers USS *Lexington* and USS *Yorktown*, and other American and Australian warships. Fletcher's mission was to prevent the Japanese convoy from reaching Port Moresby. American and Australian land-based bombing planes, in northeastern Australia and southern New Guinea, were also alerted.

The Battle of the Coral Sea began on May 7, when scouting planes from each fleet sighted some of the opposing ships. During the exchange of carrier strikes, one light Japanese carrier was sunk, and an American destroyer was also sent to the bottom by bombs. During the afternoon, Japanese land-based planes from Rabaul launched a violent attack against a force of American and Australian cruisers southwest of the Louisiade Islands, but they did not score any hits on the rapidly maneuvering ships. Not very long after this, American and Australian planes from Australia and New Guinea saw the same Allied naval squadron and thought that it was part of the Japanese force. So they, too, attacked but, like the Japanese, were unable to score any hits.

The next morning the main Japanese and American carrier forces exchanged long-range blows. Japanese planes sank the *Lexington* and slightly damaged the *Yorktown*. The American planes severely damaged the heavy carrier *Shokaku*.

By this time both sides had suffered so severely from carrier strikes

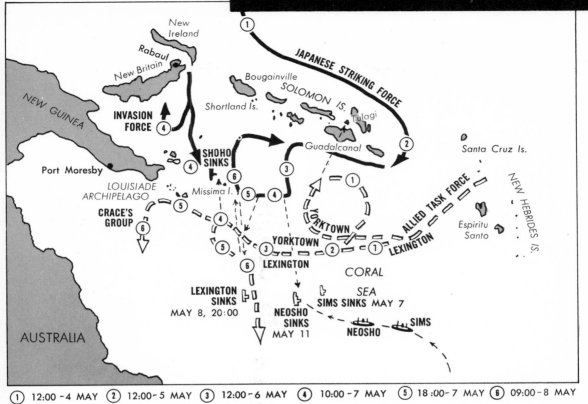

① 12:00 – 4 MAY ② 12:00 – 5 MAY ③ 12:00 – 6 MAY ④ 10:00 – 7 MAY ⑤ 18:00 – 7 MAY ⑥ 09:00 – 8 MAY

that each decided to withdraw from the fight at the same time. The commander of the Japanese expeditionary force sailing toward Port Moresby now knew that he could have no carrier protection as he approached the coast of New Guinea. Realizing that Allied bombing planes and surface ships were moving in to attack, he decided to call off the expedition. Although the battle between the two carrier forces had actually been a draw, the Americans could rightly claim that they had won a strategic victory, for they had prevented the Japanese from going to Port Moresby.

The Battle of Midway

THE JAPANESE thought they had sunk both of the American carriers in the Battle of the Coral Sea. They also knew that the carrier USS *Hornet* had been rushing down to that part of the Pacific, but had arrived too late to take part in the battle. It therefore seemed to Admiral Isoroku Yamamoto, commander of the Japanese Combined Fleet, that the time was ripe for his planned seizure of Midway. Yamamoto detached a strong force to create a diversion in the North Pacific, and at the same time to seize island bases in the Aleutians. Then, during the last days of May, he took the bulk of his fleet, many times stronger than the full force Admiral Nimitz could assemble to oppose it, toward Midway. Four carriers under Admiral Nagumo made up the main Japanese striking force. These were veterans of Pearl Harbor, Port Darwin, and the Indian Ocean raid.

But the Americans were still reading Japanese radio coded messages, and Nimitz knew Yamamoto's intentions. As the Japanese fleet began to move eastward across the Pacific, Nimitz ordered Admiral Fletcher, with the carriers *Hornet* and *Yorktown* to rush northward from the Coral Sea to meet the threat. They were joined at Pearl Harbor by the USS *Enterprise*. All three carriers, with all available cruisers and destroyers, then sailed toward Midway to wait for the Japanese.

Early on June 4, 1942, Japanese carrier aircraft delivered a heavy blow against Midway. At the same time American land-based planes from the tiny island attempted to strike back. Fifteen B-17 Flying Fortresses, and forty-five Navy and Marine Corps planes attacked the Japanese carriers. But the B-17's were flying too high to do any damage, and the faster, more maneuverable Zero carrier planes repulsed the Navy and Marine Corps attack. They shot down about half of the American planes.

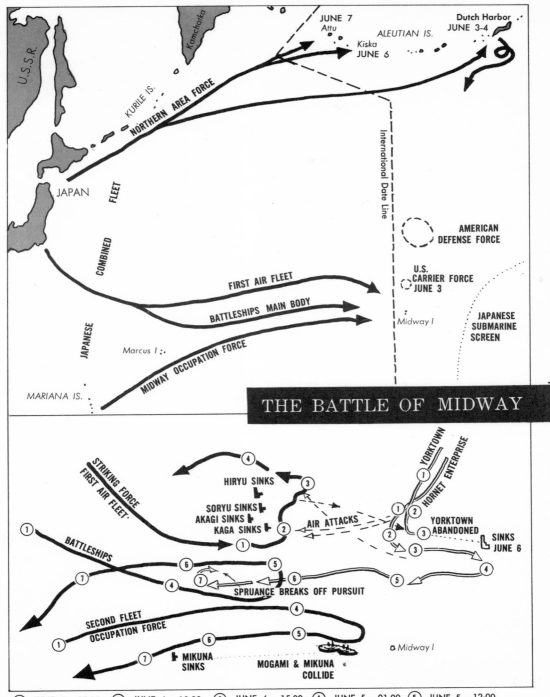

THE BATTLE OF MIDWAY

① JUNE 4 — 07:00 ② JUNE 4 — 10:00 ③ JUNE 4 — 15:00 ④ JUNE 5 — 01:00 ⑤ JUNE 5 — 12:00

⑥ JUNE 6 — 07:00 ⑦ JUNE 6 — 17:50

In midmorning the Japanese carriers were attacked by torpedo planes from the American carriers, and again the defensive fighters drove off the American planes with great loss. But immediately following this, American carrier dive bombers swept through the Japanese defensive screen in a dramatic attack, hitting three of the carriers, leaving them in a sinking condition.

A few hours later, in an exchange of carrier strikes, American pilots struck and sank the last of the Japanese heavy carriers. At the same time Japanese planes damaged the USS *Yorktown* severely. Three days later, as the crippled American carrier was being towed back to Pearl Harbor, she was torpedoed and sunk by a Japanese submarine.

But the loss of one carrier was a small price for the American fleet to pay for its success in destroying all four carriers of the main Japanese

Japanese fighter-bomber.

NAVY DEPARTMENT

striking force, and forcing Admiral Yamamoto to order a retreat. The Japanese lost 275 planes, and about half of their very best carrier pilots. The Americans lost 40 land-based planes and 92 carrier aircraft. By their victory at Midway, the Americans had ended Japanese aerial and naval domination of the ocean. This was a turning point in the Pacific war. The only Japanese accomplishment was their seizure of the tiny Aleutian islands of Attu and Kiska.

During the Battle of Midway, as in the Battle of the Coral Sea, surface vessels of the opposing sides did not see each other. The battle was fought and won completely by air power.

The Scales Tilt in the Pacific

The Fight for the Solomons

FOLLOWING THE VICTORY at Midway, the Joint Chiefs of Staff decided to attack Japanese outposts in the southern Solomon Islands. On August 7, 1942, the American 1st Marine Division landed on Guadalcanal and seized a partly completed Japanese airfield. They renamed it Henderson Field, and Army engineers rushed work to complete it for American planes. At the same time the Marines beat off repeated Japanese ground efforts to retake the field. This was the beginning of six months of bitter fighting on Guadalcanal, and on the sea and in the air nearby.

Carrier planes and surface forces on both sides took part in these battles, as did American land-based bombers from the New Hebrides

U.S. Marine SED Squadron on Guadalcanal warms up before striking at Henderson Field during December, 1942.

Islands and Japanese planes based at Rabaul in New Britain. Many of the battles took place when the Japanese tried to reinforce their troops on Guadalcanal. During most of the time this struggle for Guadalcanal was raging, both American and Japanese surface ships were careful to avoid the waters around the island during daylight, because of the danger from opposing land- and carrier-based aircraft.

On the ocean's surface, the Japanese and American navies battled each other to a standstill in a series of violent night engagements. During daylight hours, American land-based and carrier-based airplanes attacked Japanese airfields, surface convoys, and airplanes. Gradually they gained control of the air over the southern Solomons.

An important factor in their successes was the ability of the American planes to take punishment. The Japanese planes usually went down when they were hit. Once they had gained air superiority over the islands, American planes were able to strike reinforcement convoys so severely that the losses finally were heavier than the Japanese could afford. In early February, 1942, Japanese destroyers evacuated the last starving survivors of the Japanese ground garrison of Guadalcanal.

Beginning in mid-1943, American land, naval, and air forces, under the command of Admiral Halsey, began to take the offensive in the Solomons. Their advance was the right jab of a two-fisted drive, under the overall direction of General MacArthur, toward the main Japanese base at Rabaul, in New Britain.

In late June, Halsey's forces began amphibious landings on New Georgia Island, under the cover of long-range Thirteenth Air Force bombers based in the New Hebrides Islands, and shorter range Army, Navy, and Marine Corps planes from Henderson Field on Guadalcanal. After capturing New Georgia Island, the Americans continued to advance steadily in the Solomons, aided by effective air support. The last phase of the Solomons campaign began on November 1, at Empress Augusta Bay in western Bougainville. Here the Americans established a naval base and three airfields within fighter range of Rabaul itself, only 235 miles away.

American successes in the Solomons during 1943 had had several results. In the first place, instead of threatening Allied lines of communication, the Japanese had been forced back on the defensive. Secondly, in addition to the terrible losses the Japanese army had suffered in battle, about 100,000 Japanese soldiers were isolated in the Solomons, unable to take any further part in the war. And by seizing bases in the Solomons, and particularly Bougainville, the Americans were in a position to cut off the Japanese stronghold at Rabaul and to breach the main Japanese defensive perimeter.

Most important of all, the incessant air battles over the islands had cost the Japanese nearly three thousand airplanes and pilots. Japan could not afford to take such losses. Under the pressure of the continuing war, she could never again train pilots as good as those that were lost in the air struggles over the Solomon Islands.

In revetments scraped out of the palm jungle of the Solomon Islands, these B-17's await their cargo of bombs.

U.S. AIR FORCE PHOTO

Wrecked American aircraft on the Solomon Islands.

U.S. MARINE CORPS

Struggle for Papua

MEANWHILE, in mid-1942, General MacArthur's forces in New Guinea had been thrown on the defensive by a Japanese overland advance from Buna toward Port Moresby. Not until the Japanese had reached Kokoda, about thirty miles from Port Moresby, were Australian ground troops and Allied air units able to stop them. The ability of the Fifth Air Force planes to attack and cut the Japanese supply line over the mountains was a key element in this success.

In mid-September, the 7th Australian Division, supported by American and Australian air units and supplied by airdrop, began to push the Japanese slowly back over the Owen Stanley Mountains. Troop-carrying transport planes then carried the American 32nd

Division over the mountains to help the Australians drive the Japanese back into a strongly fortified coastal area around Buna and Gona. Here the Japanese held the Allies off for several months. But reinforced ground troops, aided by intensive bombing and strafing from Allied planes finally overwhelmed the Japanese defenses of Buna and Gona in January, 1943.

There was a lull in the ground fighting for nearly five months while General MacArthur waited for additional land, air and naval forces that would permit him to undertake the airborne and amphibious offensive that he and his staff had planned. Meanwhile, General George C. Kenney's Fifth Air Force had carried the war to the Japanese by repeated attacks against their strongholds around Lae and

North American B-25's, en route to bomb Rabaul, pass the invasion convoy bound for the same place. The planes, which will soften up the target for the invasion, fly several thousand feet above the ships.

Finschhafen, and their main base at Rabaul. Since the Japanese were building up their air strength in New Guinea, this had led to a series of violent air battles and to exchanges of strikes between the opposing airfields.

Battle of the Bismarck Sea

LATE IN FEBRUARY, 1943, Allied patrol planes sighted a Japanese convoy of eight small merchant ships and eight destroyers leaving Rabaul to steam westward into the Bismarck Sea. The transports were carrying about seven thousand soldiers to reinforce Lae. Because the weather was cloudy, the Japanese hoped to avoid Allied air interference, but General Kenney's medium bombers had been practicing a new method for making low-level attacks during cloudy weather. Flying just a few feet above the waves, they dropped their bombs a short distance from the target. Then, as the bombs skipped over the waves toward the enemy ship, the bombers would turn sharply away to avoid anti-aircraft fire.

On March 2, when the Japanese ships had reached a point within range of most of his medium bomber units, General Kenney ordered these units to try out their new skip-bombing method of attack. During the next three days, taking advantage of every break in the clouds, the American and Australian planes proved the method was a good one.

Japanese land-based aircraft from Rabaul tried to fly air cover over the convoy, but they were unable to interfere very effectively with the American bombers because they could not find them in or under the clouds. About twenty-five planes were shot down on each side during the intermittent air fighting that went on during the battle. During the night of March 3-4, American P-T boats entered the fight and sank one of the damaged Japanese transports.

51

U.S. medium bombers attack a Japanese merchant ship at mast height during the Battle of the Bismarck Sea.

The Battle of the Bismarck Sea ended on the following day, when American planes sank the last of the eight Japanese transports. They had also sent to the bottom four of the escorting destroyers and an auxiliary vessel. The four surviving destroyers, all damaged, returned to Rabaul. Approximately 3,000 Japanese went down with the sunken ships; about 2,700 were rescued by the surviving destroyers and by submarines.

The Japanese made no further efforts to send merchant ship convoys through the Bismarck Sea. The trickle of supplies of aviation fuel, food, equipment, and troop replacements that reached Lae were brought by fast destroyer transports that hugged the coast of New Britain or of New Guinea all the way.

Conquest of Northeast New Guinea

By June, 1943, General Kenney's airmen had won the struggle for control of the skies over the coast of northeast New Guinea. Late that same month, under an umbrella of Fifth Air Force planes, Allied troops made amphibious landings near Salamaua, the southern outpost of the Japanese strongholds around Lae. The Japanese were well protected in deep trenches and massive log bunkers cleverly concealed in the dense jungles. Under these conditions Allied airmen were unable to give much support to the ground troops. Even in those rare instances when they could see the targets, their bombings and strafings were not very effective against these excellent jungle defensive positions. The Japanese resisted fanatically, and Allied progress was slow.

Japanese planes at Rabaul made only a few efforts to interfere with the Allied air attacks; they were being kept too busy trying to oppose Halsey's advance in the Solomons. But Japanese air opposition from a base at Wewak was more effective. By the end of August, however, the Fifth Air Force had hammered Wewak so severely that the surviving Japanese planes withdrew to Hollandia, well beyond the range of Allied fighters and light bombers.

On September 4, while the Japanese were still resisting stubbornly in their defenses at Salamaua, Australian troops made an amphibious landing a few miles east of Lae. The next day, the Fifth Air Force supported an American parachute regiment in a brilliant airborne operation at Nadzab air base, nineteen miles northwest of Lae. A total of seventeen hundred men were dropped in one minute and ten seconds. These troops completely overwhelmed the surprised Japanese defenders of the field. An Australian division was immediately flown into Nadzab by air to converge with the other forces in an attack

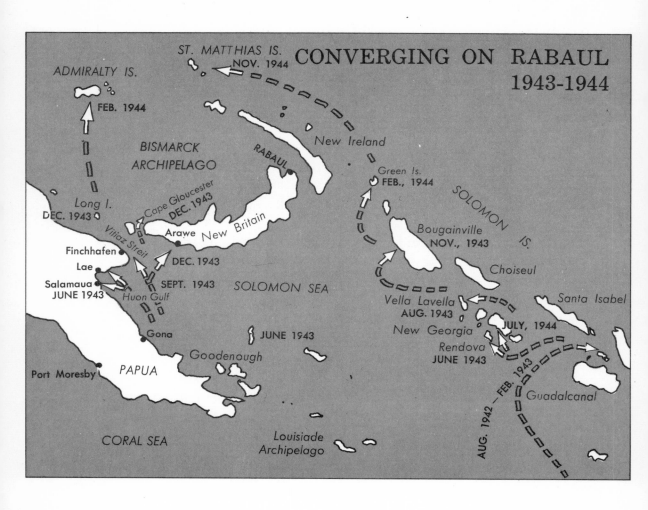

ST. MATTHIAS IS.
NOV. 1944

CONVERGING ON RABAUL
1943-1944

ADMIRALTY IS.

FEB. 1944

New Ireland

BISMARCK
ARCHIPELAGO

RABAUL

Green Is.
FEB., 1944

SOLOMON IS.

Long I.
DEC. 1943

Cape Gloucester
DEC. 1943

Bougainville
NOV., 1943

Vitiaz Strait

Arawe   New Britain

DEC. 1943

Choiseul

Finchhafen

SEPT. 1943

SOLOMON SEA

Vella Lavella
AUG. 1943

Santa Isabel

Lae

Salamaua
JUNE 1943

Huon Gulf

New Georgia

JULY, 1944

Gona

JUNE 1943

Rendova
JUNE 1943

Goodenough

PAPUA

Port Moresby

Guadalcanal

CORAL SEA

Louisiade
Archipelago

AUG. 1942 – FEB. 1943

Direct hits by B-24's, bombing from 9,500 feet, finished off this 6,000-ton Japanese merchant vessel bound for Wewak.

directly against Lae. They captured the town on September 16.

During the following months, General MacArthur's forces continued their advance up the coast of New Guinea. They captured Finschhafen on October 22, and built it into a great Allied base in preparation for the next series of operations. Providing magnificent support to the ground troops, General Kenney's Fifth Air Force developed a pattern of operations which it would continue throughout the remainder of the war.

First, fighter planes and light bombers gained air superiority over the region where the next operation was planned to take place. They did this by attacking Japanese airfields, and by trying to force Japanese planes always to fight at a disadvantage. At the same time,

Para-fragmentation bombs float down onto the parking and revetment area of the Japanese Vunakanau Field at Rabaul. Delayed action fuses on some of the bombs prevented the Japanese from going into the area for many hours.

longer range bombers neutralized distant enemy air bases, sometimes in coordination with land-based or carrier aircraft from the South or Central Pacific areas. Next, the Allied fighters and light bombers isolated the area that was to be attacked, making it impossible for Japanese troop transports or warships to land reinforcements. Finally, as General MacArthur's troops advanced on land, or prepared for an airdrop or an amphibious landing. Fifth Air Force planes intensified their attacks against ground targets in the area. These attacks continued throughout the land battle. Frequently the troops on the ground directed the bombers and fighters to their targets by means of radio messages. In an airborne operation, Fifth Air Force troop-carrying planes flew the paratroops to the objective, then shuttled back and forth to airlift reinforcements and supplies to the airborne troops.

Japanese airstrip at Lae, New Guinea, under attack by Australian and U.S. Army Air Force bombers.

A Consolidated B-24 burns after being hit by Japanese bombs.

As soon as MacArthur's forces had seized an area, they built airfields. Then fighter planes moved in to provide air support in the continuing local operations, and to carry out long-range reconnaissance and air strike in preparation for the next move. When the staffs of General MacArthur and General Kenney had completed their planning for that move, the pattern of air and surface operations would be repeated.

Fifth Air Force N-25's sweep into Rabaul Harbor at low level to turn the docks into a holocaust of fire and smoke.

Bypassing Rabaul

IN DECEMBER, 1943, land, sea, and air forces of the Southwest Pacific Theater cooperated in a series of operations that carried the ground force spearheads across Vitiaz and Dampier Straits to the southern coast of New Britain and onto nearby Long Island. Allied troops captured the Japanese airfield on Cape Gloucester on December 30, and General Kenney's planes immediately flew in to support the next landing, which was near Saidor, on the northeastern coast of New Guinea. By January 7, American and Australian planes were operating out of the Saidor airfield.

During this series of amphibious operations, General Kenney's bombers had been hammering incessantly at Rabaul, in cooperation with Admiral Halsey's Navy planes and those of the Thirteenth Air Force, from their newly captured bases on Bougainville. Allied troops made additional landings in the Green Islands on February 15, in the Admiralties on February 29, and on Emirau on March 20.

Rabaul was now surrounded. Its airfields had been so heavily pounded that they were practically useless; any Japanese planes that landed there were almost immediately destroyed on the ground. Though there were almost 100,000 Japanese soldiers left around Rabaul, they were isolated and helpless, so, with the approval of the Joint Chiefs of Staff, MacArthur decided to bypass the town. To

The Japanese found it difficult to operate from their airfield at Gasmata, New Guinea, after the American Fifth Air Force worked it over.

OFFICIAL U.S. AIR FORCE PHOTO

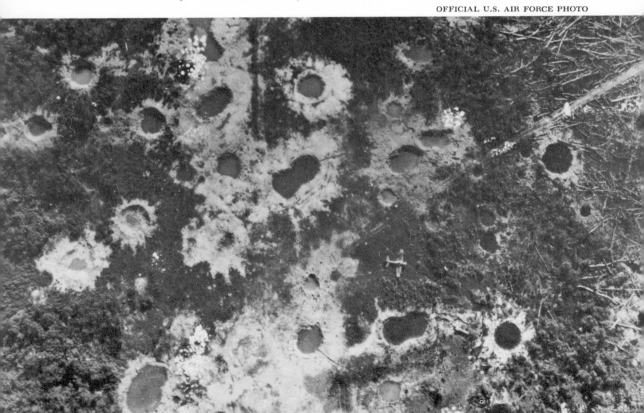

make sure that Rabaul did not recover, Thirteenth Air Force planes attacked it from time to time. At the same time, they helped the Fifth Air Force support General MacArthur's continuing operations along the New Guinea coast.

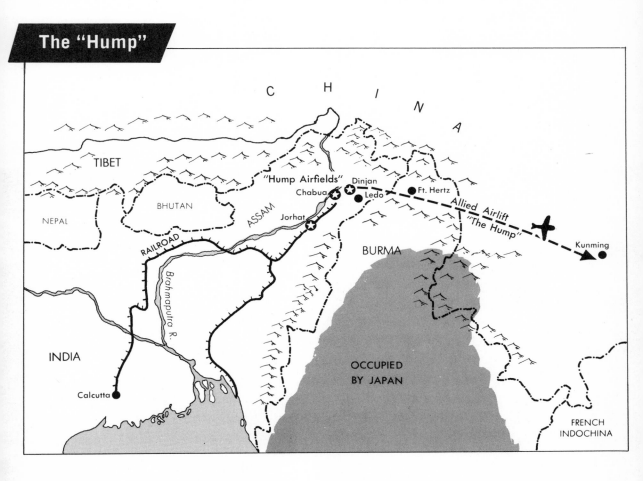

The "Hump"

Over the Hump to China

The Hump

AFTER THE JAPANESE victory in Burma, the battered survivors of the Allied ground forces made their way as best they could over the mountain ramparts around Burma into either eastern India or western China. Short of food, forced to abandon all of their heavy equipment as they followed narrow jungle trails over the mountains, these troops were kept alive only by emergency airdrops of food and other supplies by American and RAF transport planes based in India.

Laborers at Allied air base in India unload fuel that has just been flown over the "Hump."

PFJ planes of a Marine squadron on a bombing mission approach Rabaul, New Britain.

The most serious consequence of the defeat in Burma was the closing of the Burma Road. This cut off the only surface road by which supplies had reached China. The only remaining link between China and the outer world was a 500-mile air route from Assam, in northeastern India, to Kunming over a series of massive, wild mountain ranges. In late April, the American Tenth Air Force had hastily established a Ferry Command at Chabua airfield in Assam from which planes could carry critical supplies and equipment to China.

To reduce interference from Japanese fighters based at the captured airfield of Myitkyina, in northern Burma, the planes that flew to Kunming had to skirt the flank of the towering Himalayas, in southwestern Tibet, and cross the almost equally rugged mountains of northernmost Burma and western Yunnan. The lowest passes in this formidable mountain wall were 14,000 feet high. Even when flying at altitudes of 20,000 feet, the planes passed several peaks towering above them. The American pilots called this route "The Hump."

In mid-1942, there were very few transport planes available in India to fly the Hump to China. Planes were needed just as badly on other fighting fronts in Europe, in the Middle East, and in the Pacific. As a result, the few planes flying between the airfields of northeastern Assam and Kunming could bring only a pitiful trickle of supplies into China.

In Burma, the tropical rains came every day, making life miserable for everyone. Here the spinning propeller blades of a troop carrier C-47 outline arcs in the heavily moisture-laden air as the craft prepares to take off.

OFFICIAL U.S. AIR FORCE PHOTO

This C-87 has flown over the "Hump" and is in the valley on the approach to Tezpur Air Base.

The senior American officer in this part of the world was Lieutenant General Joseph W. Stilwell, a ground soldier who, early in 1942, had been sent to China as head of an American military assistance mission. Generalissimo Chiang Kai-shek had appointed Stilwell as his Chief of Staff, then sent him to command the Chinese forces that had fought in the unsuccessful battle for Burma. After the Allied defeat in Burma, Stilwell had led a group of military and civilian refugees over the mountain trails from Burma to India. Shortly after his arrival there, in July, 1942, Stilwell was placed in command of the newly created American China-Burma-India Theater of Operations, and given the job of providing support and assistance to China. At that time his only American combat troops were the few airmen of the newly created American Tenth Air Force in India. And he was still responsible in China for helping Chiang and the Chinese army leaders to build up and improve the fighting quality of their army.

Stilwell established two headquarters. One of these was in New Delhi, India, and was primarily responsible for arranging the movement of supplies over the Hump and supervising the operations of the Tenth Air Force. Stilwell's other headquarters was in Chungking, capital of China. Here his American staff took care of allocating the supplies received over the Hump, and assisted the Chinese in improving their army. In 1942 and 1943, Stilwell spent most of his time in China, where his greatest problems lay.

Weapons carrier from America being loaded aboard a C-46 plane, which will fly it over the "Hump" to China.
U.S. ARMY PHOTOGRAPH

The most difficult of these problems was the distribution of the few supplies that were arriving in Kunming over the Hump. The Chinese, desperate for supplies and equipment, did not seem to realize that Stilwell was as anxious as they were to increase this aerial flow of materials and to help China win the war. When they did not receive the things they wanted and needed, they blamed it on Stilwell, rather than on shortages of planes and pilots. As a result, Chiang Kai-shek began to feel that Stilwell was uncooperative.

The Dispute Over Tonnages

AFTER THE ALLIED DEFEAT in Burma, Chennault — now a brigadier general in the Chinese air force — had reassembled the "Flying Tigers" of his American Volunteer Group at Kunming. From the base there they protected the eastern end of the Hump aerial route and gave all possible support to Chinese ground troops engaged against the Japanese in slow-moving warfare in east and central China.

Because of the shortages of supplies being flown over the Hump, however, Chennault could not send his pilots on as many of these missions as he wished. He had to conserve his fuel for only the most important activities. Added to this, many of his planes were grounded for lack of spare parts.

Meanwhile, trouble had been brewing between Stilwell and Chennault. The two tough soldiers had liked each other when they first met, and each respected the other's ability as a fighting man. But two arguments had lately created bitterness between them.

Chennault and his Flying Tigers did not think that they were being properly treated by Stilwell's headquarters. They were particularly annoyed when they found out that they would not receive most of the supplies being brought over the Hump. They were fast using up

Japanese army "Oscar" fighter.

the scarce stocks of fuel, ammunition, and spare parts that Chennault had been able to assemble at Kunming. Chennault was afraid that his operations would come to a complete halt unless he received a much higher proportion of the Hump tonnage than Stilwell's headquarters was planning to allot him. He insisted that supplies for his planes were more important than equipment for the Chinese army.

While this argument between the two men was still going on, a second one developed. This was about the future status of the American Volunteer Group. When these men had volunteered to serve China, they had been promised excellent pay and a bonus of five hundred dollars for each Japanese plane they shot down. Since America was not at war at that time, China could not expect them to fight the Japanese and to risk their lives without a good reward. But when the

United States entered the war in December, many people had wondered about the status of the Flying Tigers. Chennault's men were receiving much more money than Army Air Force pilots who were not only taking the same risks and enduring the same hardships, but were also expected to shoot down Japanese planes without a bonus.

On the other hand, Chennault's pilots had signed contracts with the Chinese government, and these contracts would not expire until July, 1942. General Chennault had formed his Flying Tigers into the finest aerial fighting team in the world, and American military leaders did not want to break it up. They decided to keep the AVG in existence until the pilots' contracts expired. At that time, the men would be encouraged to volunteer to join the Army Air Force and to continue fighting the Japanese in China.

A Japanese battery of 105's being fired in the China war zone.

WIDE WORLD PHOTO

Chennault and many of his men fully agreed that they should not be receiving special treatment, and higher rates of pay, than other American fighting men doing the same kind of job. Chennault personally agreed at once to return to the Army Air Force as a brigadier general and to take a decrease in pay. But because they felt Stilwell had not supported them, most of the Flying Tigers decided they would not fight under him, even though they wanted to remain with Chennault. Only five of the AVG veterans volunteered to stay in China; nearly sixty decided to go home.

Fearful that Allied air strength in China would collapse, the Army Air Force rushed a number of pilots to China. There, in July, 1942, these pilots joined the remaining AVG veterans in the newly established China Air Task Force under Chennault's command. In the following months, under Chennault's leadership, and following his combat methods, the China Air Task Force was just as successful against the Japanese as the Flying Tigers had been.

The success of the new task force, however, did not end the dispute between Stilwell and Chennault. They continued to argue over the distribution of supplies coming over the Hump. Chennault felt that he and his pilots had proven themselves greatly superior to the Japanese air force. He believed that if he had enough fuel and ammunition, his air task force could defeat the Japanese air force in China, and that he would then be able to bomb and strafe the Japanese ground troops right out of the country. He saw no reason why the limited capacity of the Hump should be used to build up Chinese ground forces, for he did not think that they would be needed.

Stilwell, on the other hand, insisted that air attacks alone would not halt the Japanese; Chinese ground troops must also be strengthened. He believed that the Japanese would try to capture the American bases by ground attacks as soon as they were seriously bothered

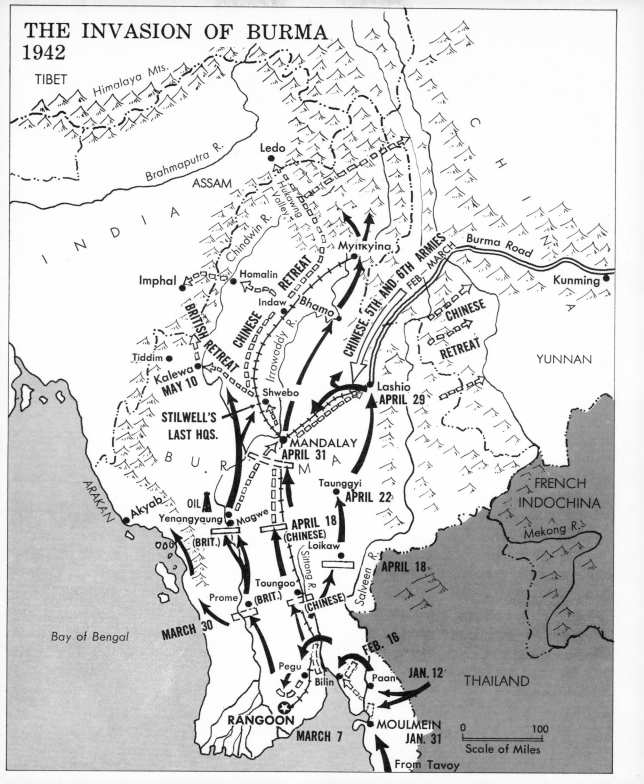

THE INVASION OF BURMA
1942

TIBET

Himalaya Mts.

Brahmaputra R.

ASSAM

Ledo

Hukawng Valley

Chindwin R.

I N D I A

Imphal

Homalin

Indaw

Myitkyina

Bhamo

Irrawaddy R.

CHINESE RETREAT

CHINESE 5TH AND 6TH ARMIES FEB.—MARCH

C H I N A

Burma Road

Kunming

YUNNAN

Tiddim

Kalewa
MAY 10

BRITISH RETREAT

Shwebo

Lashio
APRIL 29

CHINESE RETREAT

STILWELL'S
LAST HQS.

MANDALAY
APRIL 31

B U R M A

Taunggyi
APRIL 22

FRENCH
INDOCHINA

Mekong R.

ARAKAN

Akyab

OIL

Yenangyaung

Magwe

APRIL 18
(CHINESE)

Loikaw

APRIL 18

(BRIT.)

Salveen R.

Bay of Bengal

Toungoo
(BRIT.)

Prome

Sittang R.

(CHINESE)

MARCH 30

FEB. 16

JAN. 12

THAILAND

Pegu

Bilin

Paan

RANGOON

MARCH 7

MOULMEIN
JAN. 31

0   100
Scale of Miles

From Tavoy

Allied flyers called this Japanese prewar Kawaski bomber "Mary." It was used mainly in China during the war, where its water-cooled engines caused much trouble in combat.

U.S. NAVY DEPARTMENT

by Chennault's air operations. Unless the Chinese ground forces were greatly improved, they would be unable to halt such Japanese drives. Furthermore, Stilwell claimed, he needed a well-equipped ground army to help reopen a land supply route through Burma in order to get additional supplies for both the ground and air units in China.

Stilwell, therefore, ordered the Hump airlift to divide its loads between ground equipment and Air Force supplies and fuel. Chiang Kai-shek agreed with Chennault. But in Washington, American Generals Marshall and Arnold felt that Stilwell was right. And so the supplies came in as Stilwell had ordered — for a while.

Creation of the Fourteenth Air Force

EARLY IN 1943, Chinese diplomatic pressure, added to the arguments of Chennault's friends in the United States, finally convinced President Roosevelt that Chennault should be given a chance to prove what he could do with air power. Roosevelt had Chennault promoted to major general, and on March 10, 1943, the China Air Task Force became the Fourteenth Air Force. At the same time, the Joint Chiefs of Staff ordered Stilwell to see to it that as much Hump tonnage as possible went to Chennault's air units.

In the light of these instructions from the Joint Chiefs of Staff, Stilwell gave Chennault an almost free hand in operating the new air force. As additional transport airplanes finally began to arrive from the United States, the amount of materials flown over the Hump increased steadily from about 3,000 tons per month in the late summer of 1942 to nearly 7,000 tons per month by the fall of 1943. With more gasoline and ammunition and fighter planes, the Fourteenth Air Force soon gained air control over central China. Chennault then began to deploy his expanded fighter forces to fields farther east, beyond Kweilin.

Meanwhile, Chennault continued to receive reports from his efficient Chinese air-warning net. The Japanese made few air moves that were not struck down by the Fourteenth Air Force fighters. As a result, the Americans extended their air superiority over eastern China. Chennault's new bombers also began to harass Japanese shipping on the China Sea, and to strike heavy blows against the main Japanese-occupied areas in eastern and northern China and even against Formosa. At last things were looking up for the Allies in China.

Arrival of the B-29's

AT THE CAIRO CONFERENCE in December, 1943, Prime Minister

Japanese "Nick" fighter potholed by pieces of a fragmentation bomb delivered in a low altitude attack on a Japanese airfield.

Churchill and Generalissimo Chiang Kai-shek agreed to an American proposal to use airfields in India and China as bases for operations of new Amercan B-29 "Superfortress" bombers. These powerful, heavily armed planes could fly over 350 miles per hour, and could carry 20,000 pounds of bombs against targets over 1,500 miles from their bases. In April and May of 1944, the first B-29's began to fly from the United States to airfields in India, near Calcutta. Their first combat mission took place on June 5, 1944: an attack on railway targets at Bangkok, in Thailand. Immediately after this, the great planes flew from India to Chengtu, in western China, where Chinese coolies, under the supervision of American engineers, had built five fields with extra-long runways.

74

Scores and scores of Chinese men and women laborers pull a 10-ton roller, mashing mud, stones, and gravel into a solid, mile-long runway for the B-29's in China.

On June 15, 1944, sixty-eight B-29's took off from the fields around Chengtu to hit a steel plant on the southernmost Japanese island of Kyushu. This was the first American attack against the home islands of Japan since Doolittle's small-scale, hit-and-run bomb raid, more than two years earlier.

Because of the limitations on the total amount of supplies and equipment that could be carried over the Hump, the B-29's were based permanently near Calcutta. Thus barracks, repair shops, and heavy support equipment could be kept in India, where they would not interfere with the regular Hump airlift. The B-29's themselves ferried their own fuel and bombs from India to Chengtu. Then, to be able to reach southern Japan, the bombers would fly from Calcutta to Chengtu to refuel and load their bombs. In between these raids on Japan, the great planes attacked Japanese bases in Southeast Asia from their fields near Calcutta.

Into the Western Pacific

The Far Eastern Air Forces in New Guinea

AFTER THE SOLOMONS and Papua had been captured by the Americans, the Japanese had drawn back their defensive perimeter to establish a new line through the Marianas and the Carolines to northwestern New Guinea. Intending to prevent a repetition of their defeat at Rabaul, they had hurriedly built up several airfields near Hollandia, from which they expected to be able to strike Allied troops advancing along the coast of New Guinea. At the same time, the Japanese reinforced their Eighteenth Army so as to hold positions between Madang

Bomb and storage dump under attack by Fifth Air Force planes at Wewak, New Guinea.

and Wewak. These positions could be supported by Japanese fighters and bombers from the Hollandia fields.

General MacArthur decided to make his next blow directly at Hollandia, even though this was 500 miles from his nearest airfields, and far beyond the range of his fighter units. The Japanese never thought he would risk an amphibious landing without fighter cover and support over the beachhead, but at MacArthur's request, Admiral Nimitz sent the Fast Carrier Task Force, under Vice Admiral Marc Mitscher, to provide air cover for an amphibious landing at Hollandia. Because of the danger of operating carrier forces close to land and land-based aircraft, however, Nimitz told MacArthur that the carriers could stay near the coast of New Guinea for only three days.

Japanese stronghold at Hollandia, New Guinea, after being bombed by U.S. aircraft.

Three days were enough. While two Allied divisions were landing near Hollandia, two regiments made another landing at Aitape, farther east, midway between the Japanese Eighteenth Army and its Hollandia base. Allied troops seized airfields at Aitape and put them into operation two days later. Before the American carriers had to withdraw from the coast of Hollandia, General Kenney's land-based fighters from Aitape were providing air cover and support for the troops attacking Hollandia, and also for the amphibious forces offshore.

Japanese air force units in northern New Guinea tried to strike back at the Allied beachheads. But the speed and smooth efficiency of the Allied operation, combined with the growing Allied superiority in numbers, skill, and experience, put the Japanese airmen at a terrible disadvantage. Their losses were heavy, while those of the Americans were light. By the time the Aitape-Hollandia operations were over, Japanese army air units in northern New Guinea were practically wiped out. The Japanese had lost almost all of their remaining experienced army pilots, which meant that they were unable to provide any other effective resistance in the air to the continued Allied movement along the coast of New Guinea. By the end of the summer, General MacArthur's force controlled the entire northern coast of the island.

A few of the 101 Wakde-based planes destroyed by U.S. Navy bombs on April 21, 1944.

The Carriers in the Central Pacific

AFTER THE BATTLE OF MIDWAY, the United States had been left with only three operational heavy carriers in the Pacific. These were capable of carrying a total of about 250 combat planes. Though the Japanese had twice as many carriers and carrier air groups, their losses in the Indian Ocean, in the Battle of the Coral Sea, and at Midway had seriously reduced the number of their best-trained and most skilled carrier pilots. Japanese superiority in the Central Pacific was severely threatened.

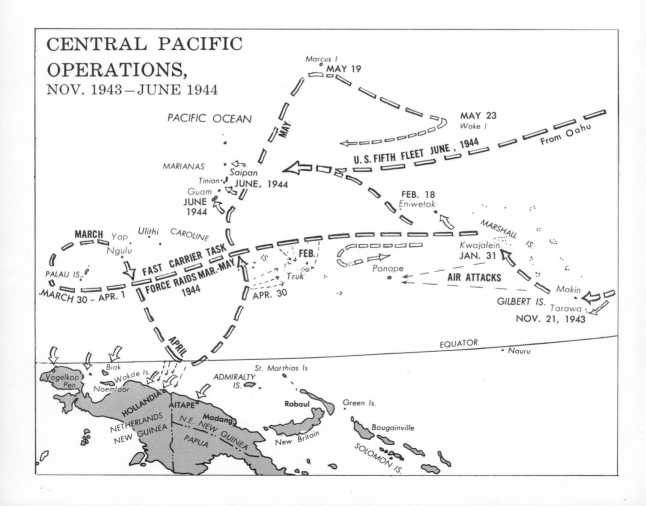

CENTRAL PACIFIC OPERATIONS, NOV. 1943 – JUNE 1944

At that time, the United States had three more carriers in the Atlantic, and these were soon sent to the Pacific by way of the Panama Canal. Also, a number of new carriers were rushed to completion in American shipyards on the Atlantic, Pacific, and Gulf of Mexico coasts. Most important, however, was the fact that the Americans, with their efficient naval air training program, were producing first-rate carrier pilots much faster than were the Japanese.

Even more serious for the Japanese were the losses their navy air force had suffered in 1943, during the day-in, day-out struggles in the air over the Solomons. In an effort to reverse the trend of the battle, in early 1943 Admiral Yamamoto had shifted some of his very best remaining carrier groups from his carriers at Truk to the bases at Rabaul and the northern Solomons. There were not enough of these groups, however, and the Japanese Zero fighter planes, although they were faster and more maneuverable than those of the Americans, had simply been unable to stand up in the wear and tear of the daily fighting. Furthermore, American planes from New Guinea and the Solomons had kept up a steady pounding of the Japanese airfields around Rabaul, destroying many of the Japanese planes on the ground.

Soon after this, Admiral Yamamoto himself became a victim of American air power. On April 18, 1943, he flew to Bougainville on an inspection trip. But American radios intercepted messages about this visit, and as Yamamoto's plane came in for a landing, it was shot down by American fighter planes waiting overhead. Yamamoto was killed.

By the end of 1943, after the grueling battles over the Solomons, the Japanese navy air force had lost approximately 3,000 planes. American losses had been less than 1,000, and American factories were turning out replacement planes more rapidly than the Japanese; American training schools were also producing pilots more quickly.

By late 1943, therefore, although the Japanese navy had still retained a strong force of aircraft carriers, it had very few trained carrier flyers for these vessels. Accordingly, during the last months of 1943 and the beginning of 1944 the Japanese withdrew their carriers from the Southwest Pacific, and began an intensive replacement training program to build up new carrier air groups which they hoped would be able again to fight the Americans on even terms sometime before the end of 1944.

The American situation was far different. By the fall of 1943, Admiral Nimitz' Fast Carrier Task Force consisted of twelve carriers, carrying nearly eight hundred combat planes. Beginning in November of 1943, this task force swept the waters of the Central Pacific in support of amphibious operations in the Gilbert and Marshall Islands. They then began to carry out long-range raids against distant Japanese air and naval bases as far west as the Palau Islands. And in between these raids, in April, 1944, the carrier task force also came down to assist Southwest Pacific Theater forces in their campaign against Hollandia.

Battle of the Philippine Sea

IN JUNE, 1944, Admiral Spruance led his Fifth Fleet to spearhead the invasion of the Marianas Islands. By this time the Fast Carrier Task Force, now commanded by Admiral Marc A. Mitscher, consisted of sixteen carriers and more than nine hundred planes.

When the Americans invaded the Marianas, Admiral Soemu Toyoda — now commanding the Japanese Combined Fleet — decided that he must try to fight back. Although the newly trained carrier groups were not as ready for combat as he wanted them to be, Toyoda still felt that they had a good chance of success in a major naval battle near the Marianas. The Japanese Mobile Force, including nine

Bomb craters pockmark the New Guinea airdrome on Wewak after a raid by U.S. bombers. More than 150 Japanese aircraft were destroyed, along with 300 flight crews and ground personnel.

Japanese carriers, had 473 combat planes. Toyoda, and Vice Admiral Jisaburo Ozawa, direct commander of the Mobile Force, were counting on assistance from about 500 land-based planes on the fields in the Marianas.

The result was the two-day Battle of the Philippine Sea, which began on June 19, 1944. Taking advantage of the longer range of his carrier planes, Ozawa sent them on a strike against the Fifth Fleet from a distance of 300 miles, which was too far away for the slower, shorter-range American planes to hit back at the Japanese carriers. Not only did Ozawa expect assistance from planes in the Marianas, he also planned to have his own planes refuel and load more ammunition on Guam. Then they would hit the American fleet again, on their way back to their own carriers. But it did not work out quite that way.

In the first place, in the days immediately before the Japanese fleet sailed out to fight, the American carrier planes had hammered the Marianas airfields so heavily that most of the Japanese planes based there were destroyed. In addition, to prevent reinforcements from reaching the Marianas from Japan, one carrier group had also smashed Japanese airfields in the Bonin and Volcano islands. Thus Ozawa could not obtain the land-based air support he had expected for the battle.

In addition, the poorly trained Japanese carrier pilots straggled into the battle in widely separated, uncoordinated groups. Most of the attacking planes were shot down by the waiting American fighters before they got close to the American fleet; few of those that reached the ships were able to get through the intense antiaircraft fire.

In that one day of aerial combat, 402 Japanese planes were destroyed, while only 26 American planes were lost — and half of the shot-down American airmen were rescued. American flyers called this one-sided air battle "the Marianas Turkey Shoot."

After this disaster, Ozawa retreated with his fleet. Spruance pursued at full speed during the night of June 19-20. Next day, Admiral Mitscher sent his planes on a daring, long-range strike against the Japanese fleet, even though it was still beyond the theoretical range of his planes. As a result, they sank several Japanese ships and destroyed 22 more Japanese planes, while 20 of their own aircraft were shot down. On the way back from this strike, 80 American planes ran out of gas and either dropped into the ocean or crash-landed on their carriers, attempting to land with their last drop of gas. As a result approximately 200 American airmen were lost in the water; but of these, 150 were rescued either during the night or early the next morning.

The two-day Battle of the Philippine Sea resulted in the loss of practically all of the newly trained Japanese carrier air groups. This was an air power loss from which Japan never recovered. The battle also assured American capture of the Marianas, thus cutting the Japanese perimeter. These islands, furthermore, were less than 1,500 miles from Japan; within the range of the new Superfortresses.

A new, and final, stage of the war was about to begin.

Index